T0001282

HOW DO WE COMMUNICATE?

THIS EDITION
Editorial Management by Oriel Square
Produced for DK by WonderLab Group LLC
Jennifer Emmett, Erica Green, Kate Hale, *Founders*

Editors Grace Hill Smith, Libby Romero, Michaela Weglinski;
Photography Editors Kelley Miller, Annette Kiesow, Nicole di Mella; **Managing Editor** Rachel Houghton;
Designers Project Design Company; **Researcher** Michelle Harris; **Copy Editor** Lori Merritt;
Indexer Connie Binder; **Proofreader** Larry Shea; **Reading Specialist** Dr. Jennifer Albro;
Curriculum Specialist Elaine Larson

Published in the United States by DK Publishing
1745 Broadway, 20th Floor, New York, NY 10019

Copyright © 2023 Dorling Kindersley Limited
DK, a Division of Penguin Random House LLC
23 24 25 26 10 9 8 7 6 5 4 3 2 1
001-333986-June/2023

A catalog record for this book
is available from the Library of Congress.
HC ISBN: 978-0-7440-7323-2
PB ISBN: 978-0-7440-7324-9

DK books are available at special discounts when purchased in bulk for sales promotions, premiums,
fundraising, or educational use. For details, contact: DK Publishing Special Markets,
1745 Broadway, 20th Floor, New York, NY 10019
SpecialSales@dk.com

Printed and bound in China

The publisher would like to thank the following for their kind permission to reproduce their images:
a=above; c=center; b=below; l=left; r=right; t=top; b/g=background

123RF.com: fxegs / F. Javier Espuny 23crb; **Alamy Stock Photo:** Niels Poulsen 26br;
Dorling Kindersley: Museum of Design in Plastics, Bournemouth Arts University, UK / Gary Ombler 26bl,
National Museum of Wales / Dave King 21b, University of Aberdeen / Gary Ombler 22b; **Dreamstime.com:** Noam Armonn 7b,
Yuriy Chaban 23tr, Feverpitched 11tr, Golfxx 16br, Handmademedia 10crb, Ayse Ezgi Icmeli 6cb, Jcpjr 14clb, Mcpics 1cb,
Monkey Business Images 4-5, 28-29, Ian Poole 24cb, Andrey Popov 8crb, Alexei Poselenov 14br, Prostockstudio 9cr,
Paulus Rusyanto 9cl, Suse Schulz 20br, Anchalee Yates 15crb, Vladyslava Yakovenko 7ca, Yobro10 11b;
Getty Images / iStock: DigitalVision Vectors / Nastasic 27tr

Cover images: *Front:* **Shutterstock.com:** aappp c, b/g; *Spine:* **Shutterstock.com:** aappp

All other images © Dorling Kindersley
For more information see: www.dkimages.com

For the curious
www.dk.com

HOW DO WE COMMUNICATE?

Libby Romero

Contents

6   Spread the Word

10   Types of Communication

16   Sending and Receiving Messages

20 The History of Communication

30 Glossary

31 Index

32 Quiz

Spread the Word

Hi! My name is Libby. I wrote this book. It's nice to meet you. Do you know what I'm doing right now? I'm communicating with you! That's right. I wrote down a thought, and you read it.
That's communication!

Communication is a long word, but all it means is sharing a thought or idea with someone else. Writing is just one way people communicate. For example, if someone wants to say "Hello" to a friend, they might write, speak, wave, or even send a waving hand emoji 👋🏻 in a text or email.

It is possible to communicate with people on the other side of the world using a computer.

To communicate, people need a few basic things: a sender, a receiver, and a message. They also need a way to send the message—such as a letter or a text message. And both people need to understand the message. For instance, they speak the same language, or they can both interpret the secret code.

How does someone know if a message was a success? The receiver responds to the message. That reaction is called feedback. Altogether, this process is how communication works.

More Ways to Communicate
Wearing hearing aids helps people with hearing loss communicate with others. People within the Deaf community can read lips or use American Sign Language (ASL). ASL is a visual language that uses hand movements and facial expressions to convey information.

How Communication Works

A sender and a receiver must understand each other for a message to be a success.

Types of Communication

Verbal Communication

Studies show that people spend up to 80 percent of their day communicating with others. They do that in a few different ways.

One obvious way people communicate is by talking with friends, family, teachers, neighbors, and others. This is called verbal communication.

Talking Time
The average person speaks about 7,000 words a day. Some people talk even more than that!

The Art of Listening

Listening is a very important part of communication. Ears constantly pick up information. People really need to focus on what they hear—or truly listen—to understand a verbal message.

Talking is one way to share information.

Nonverbal Communication

As much as people tend to talk, words are only part of how we communicate. Our bodies speak, too! This is called body language, and it's a kind of nonverbal communication.

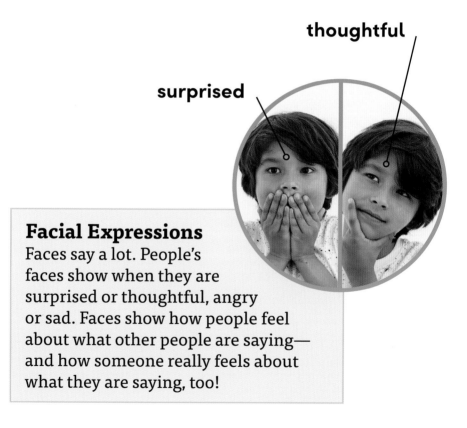

thoughtful

surprised

Facial Expressions
Faces say a lot. People's faces show when they are surprised or thoughtful, angry or sad. Faces show how people feel about what other people are saying— and how someone really feels about what they are saying, too!

When people talk, their bodies move.
Their hands move. Their eyes move.
Each of these movements adds meaning
to a conversation.

angry

happy

Written Communication

Another way to send a message is to write it down. People write letters, texts, social media posts, blogs, and emails. They can write a thank-you note to a friend. Or they can write a letter to their state representative about an important issue. That's a good way to make sure that person listens to what someone has to say.

There are lots of ways to write messages— like this message in the sky!

This message is clear: this car is dirty!

Visual Communication

People also communicate with visuals. These are things like pictures, videos, charts, and symbols. Visuals are a quick and easy way to send a message. They take complex ideas and present them in a way that most people can understand. Visual messages are all around us. They keep us informed.

This symbol means "Don't Walk." It means that it is not yet safe to walk.

The Power of Pictures
The human brain processes visual information 60,000 times faster than it interprets written words.

Sending and Receiving Messages

The human body is an amazing machine. It allows people to talk or use gestures so they can send messages to each other. It also has the tools needed to understand all of the messages coming in. Let's find out how it does this!

How do people talk? It starts with the lungs. Puffs of air move up from the lungs to the larynx, or voice box. This causes the vocal chords to vibrate and make sound. The throat, mouth, tongue, and lips work together to transform those sounds into words and sentences.

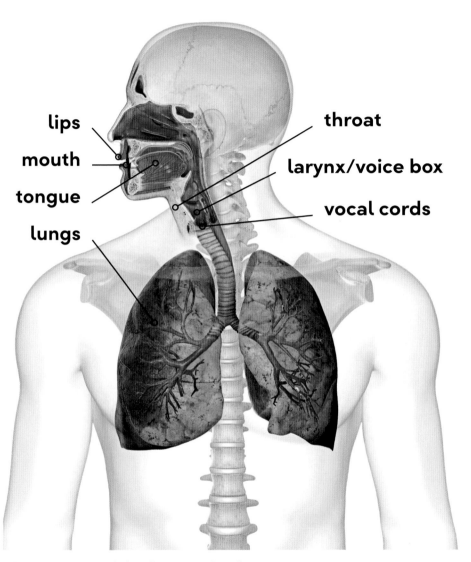

lips

mouth

tongue

lungs

throat

larynx/voice box

vocal cords

These parts of the human body help people communicate.

How do eyes interpret visual messages? Very quickly! Imagine a person at a crosswalk. Light bounces off the sign, enters the cornea, passes through the pupil, and reaches the lens. The lens focuses the light onto the retina, which takes a picture of the sign and sends it to the brain. In an instant, that person knows it's time to cross the street. When the sign changes, it also beeps. This is another signal that it's safe to walk across the street.

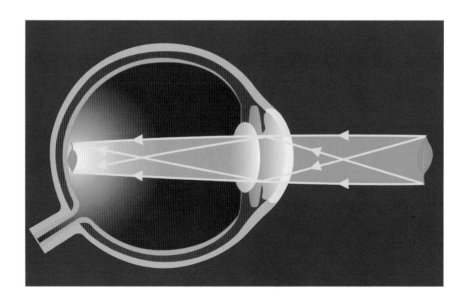

How do people hear those beeps at the crosswalk? The sound moves from the outer ear, through the ear canal, to the eardrum, which vibrates. The vibrations hit three tiny bones in the middle ear—the malleus, incus, and stapes—and move on to the cochlea in the inner ear. The cochlea is filled with fluid. As the fluid moves, it activates nerve endings. They change the vibrations into electrical impulses that travel through a nerve to the brain. The brain interprets this as sound.

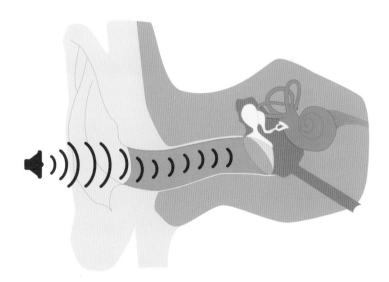

The History of Communication

As long as there have been people on Earth, they have communicated with each other. Ancient people told stories. They drew and painted pictures, too. A cave in France, for example, is filled with prehistoric drawings and paintings of animals, symbols, and mythological creatures. The paintings date back to around 15,000 BCE. Archaeologists think they were made either to tell stories or to send messages about the best places for hunting.

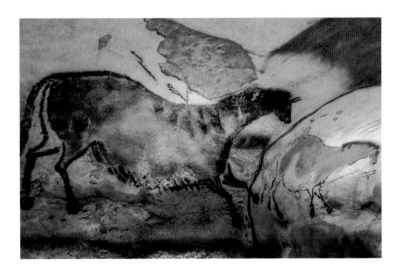

There are prehistoric paintings and engravings of deer, bison, and wild cats on the walls and ceiling of the Lascaux Cave in southern France.

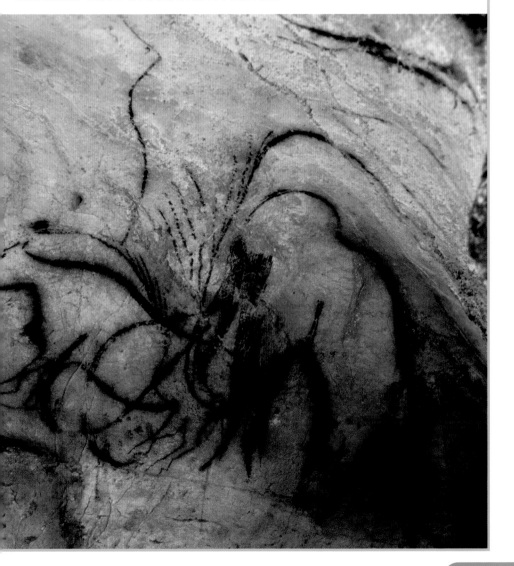

Written language first emerged around 3200 BCE. People in Mesopotamia were growing and trading lots of animals and crops. They needed a way to keep track of everything, so they invented the first system of writing called cuneiform. Egyptians then created a form of writing called hieroglyphics about 50 years later. Over time, other places around the world invented their own forms of writing, too.

Mesopotamian scribes used reeds to write on clay cuneiform tablets.

For centuries, people wrote everything down by hand. That took a long time. Then, in 868 CE, Chinese inventors made the first printing press to speed things up.

More than 500 years later, in 1450 CE, German inventor Johannes Gutenberg invented a new printing press with moveable type. This invention made it cheaper, faster, and easier to communicate in writing than ever before.

Unlocking Hieroglyphics

Ancient Egyptian priests wrote using symbols called hieroglyphics. Over time, they stopped using them, and people forgot what the symbols meant. In 1799, someone discovered a stone slab covered with ancient writing in three languages: hieroglyphics, ancient Greek, and Demotic. Scientists called it the Rosetta Stone, and they used it to figure out what the hieroglyphics meant.

The problem was that a newspaper or book could only be read by one person at a time. What if someone wanted to quickly spread a message to lots of people at once over a long distance?

Enter the telegraph! In 1844, Samuel Morse sent the first message through wires with his new invention. In just six years, telegraph lines followed the railroads as they made their way across the country.

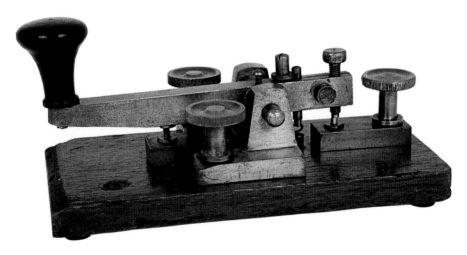

The telegraph used electricity to transfer coded messages across wires. The messages were written using a system of dots and dashes.

But it didn't take long for something even better to come along. In 1876, Alexander Graham Bell introduced the telephone. Now, people could actually to talk to each other when they were in different places. A year later, Bell invented the first phonograph. With it, people could record sounds that they could listen to later.

Several other scientists claimed to have invented the first telephone. Alexander Graham Bell gets the credit because he was the first to receive a patent, which gave him the right to sell the device.

A Royal Telegram

In 1858, Great Britain's Queen Victoria sent a telegram to U.S. president James Buchanan. It was the first telegram to cross the Atlantic Ocean. It took almost 16 hours for her message to reach him, but it would have taken at least 10 days by ship!

In the 20th century, mass communications changed the world. Radio was invented, and it quickly became a popular source for up-to-date news and entertainment. Movie theaters sprung up all over the world. The first television was invented in 1927, but it would be decades later before TVs were common in people's homes. Telecommunications emerged in the 20th century, too. Computers and mobile phones revolutionized how we communicate.

Using the radio dial, people could tune in to music, news, stories, and live broadcasts.

Early televisions only worked in black-and-white.

Moving Pictures

Technically, the first motion picture was created in 1877. It consisted of 12 photos, taken as a racehorse ran around a track. When the photos were placed on a rotating disk and projected onto a screen, it looked like the horse was running.

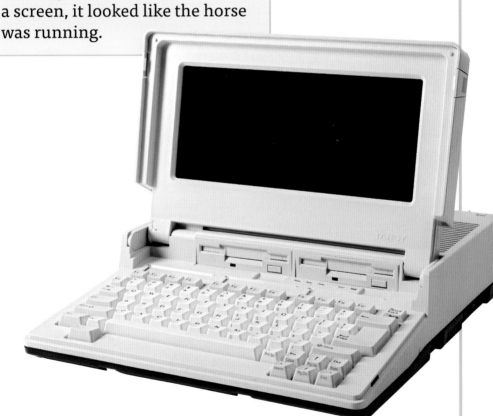

Made in the 1980s, the Tandy 1400 was one of the first laptop computers that worked with PC software programs.

All of this leads up to the time we live in today: **the Information Age**. Most people don't have to be in the same room to communicate face-to-face anymore. They can talk to each other online. People share information about their lives on social media. There are endless ways to communicate in the 21st century.

Well, we're at the end of the book. If I did my job as a writer, I communicated my message and you're still with me! Hopefully, you have a better understanding of what communication is and how it has changed over time. **Mission accomplished!**

Kids can communicate through video games, mobile phones, and other devices. Remember to check with an adult before logging on to a new website or app.

Glossary

Body language
The posture, gestures, and facial expressions that are a part of nonverbal communication

Communication
The act of transmitting a message

Cuneiform
An ancient form of writing, developed by ancient Sumerians in Mesopotamia, that used wedge-shaped characters

Feedback
When someone gives back opinions, corrections, or comments

Gestures
Movements of the face or body that express or emphasize a feeling or idea

Hieroglyphics
Ancient Egyptian writing that uses pictures and symbols to represent words

Information Age
The modern age where information moves quickly, especially through computers

Mass communication
The sending or receiving of messages to many people at once

Nonverbal communication
The sending or receiving of silent messages

Verbal communication
The sending or receiving of messages with sound

Index

American Sign
Language (ASL) 8

ancient people 20–23

Bell, Alexander
Graham 25

body language 12–13

Buchanan, James 25

communication
process 8–9

computers 7, 26, 27

cuneiform 22

Deaf community 8

ears 19

eyes 18

facial expressions 12

feedback 8, 9

Gutenberg, Johannes
23

hieroglyphics 22, 23

history of
communication
20–29

human body 16–19

Information Age 28

listening 11

mass communication
28–29

Morse, Samuel 24

motion pictures 27

nonverbal
communication
12–13

phonograph 25

prehistoric
communication
20–21

printing press 23

radio 26

sending and receiving
messages 16–19

talking 10–11, 16

telegrams 25

telegraph 24

telephone 25, 26

television 26

types of
communication
10–15

verbal communication
10–11

Victoria, Queen of
Great Britain 25

visual communication
15, 18

written communication
7, 14

Quiz

Answer the questions to see what you have learned. Check your answers in the key below.

1. What are three basic things you need to communicate?

2. Talking is what kind of communication?

3. What kind of communication uses body language?

4. What was the first form of writing called?

5. Pick one invention mentioned in the book. How did it change the way people communicate?

1. A sender, a receiver, and a message 2. Verbal 3. Nonverbal communication 4. Cuneiform 5. Answers will vary